PATH OF HOPE:

Difficult Experiences and Challenges in Dark Times
of Drug Trafficking, all going on around her.

Esperanza Gutierrez Piñeros

Esperanza Gutierrez Piñeros

PATH OF HOPE

Difficult Experiences and Challenges in Dark Times
of Drug Trafficking, all going on around her

DEDICATION

Dedicated to those who have faced the darkest shadows of life and have found the strength to move forward. To God, who has been my constant guide and the light that has illuminated my path in the most painful moments. To my family and friends, who have sustained me with unconditional love and have been my earthly angels. "May this account of personal experiences be a spark of hope for all, reminding us that even in the deepest despair, faith in God is the beacon that leads us day by day to maintain inner peace.

To those whose hearts have been touched by sadness and adversity, I hope these pages bring you comfort and show you that, in the midst of darkness, the divine light of hope always shines brightly. With gratitude and love.

Hope

INDEX

CHAPTER 1

My Journey from Girl to Woman

In the Garden of Childhood, there lived a little girl whose name radiated hope. With her heart full of illusions and her mind full of fairy tales, she discovered a magical world through black and white television, letting her imagination fly towards unknown horizons.

She also enjoyed the rare moments when her mother, Alicia, was in a good mood to tell them about the life of her ancestors. They belonged to the Spanish Royalty, and Alicia would narrate the majesty of their palaces, where her grandmother had grown up. She described the beautiful long dresses they dragged along the floor as they descended the stairs, as well as the delicate materials from which they were made. However, her grandfather, a military man of prestige, had a penchant for gambling and in those days, perhaps still considered, a man's word had value. Gambling debts were called debts of honor, which led to the loss of all the grandmother's assets. They even came to have to pay with houses, land and even slaves. Alicia grew up in financial straits. At the age of 14, she met a handsome young man and decided to get married at that young age. Despite warnings from her family, who told her that marrying this man would mean losing her family forever, she stuck to her idea and so it was... she never saw them again."

Now, Esperanza, one of the many children that Alicia had, had to stop fantasizing to face a reality in which she only saw around her hostility, suffering, scarcity, contrariness, discomfort and many people who could not manage to agree on anything. Every morning was one of shouting and fighting, since everyone was in a hurry and there was only one bathroom.
Esperanza, in her innocence, thought it was normal. She tried to understand the point of view of each of her siblings, constantly observing their behavior and then understanding why Alicia, their mother, gave them strong reprimands. Most of the time there was no father, and it was better that he was not at home. When he arrived, a real catastrophe was unleashed.

Everyone began to tremble and fear invaded them. Some hid in the closets, others under the beds, but it was useless to hide, since they had to come out and say hello anyway, as he began to call their names one by one. We had to approach him in silence, trying to hide our panic.

That father was not an alcoholic, but something worse than that: he was irresponsible and disrespectful, without any education. Several times Alicia tried to talk to the director of some institution, or to the manager of some company, even to the minister, in order to get a job for her husband. Finally, when they succeeded, they sent him to work in another city and he left. After two or three months, Alicia went to ask when her husband would be back and was asked, "Are you Alicia? The company had financed their move and provided them with tickets to get everyone settled there. It turned out that he had moved in with another woman with whom he also had children. That was the kind of person, rather, individual, for whom Alicia had left her family."

Supposedly, this was a Catholic family; they went to mass every Sunday, but they did not know GOD. When they left church and returned home, they were still confrontational, rude in the way they expressed themselves and beat their wives. I say this in the plural because there were older sons who were already married and who followed their father's example.

Esperanza missed one of her brothers, who studied at a boarding school and could only see him on special occasions. At her first communion, he attended the celebration and they managed to take a picture together, saying, This moment we will remember forever, as if we were a couple in their marriage. Truly, this brother has been unparalleled, not only for her, but also for her sisters and brothers. Throughout Esperanza's journey, he has been her unconditional support, always giving her good things. He would tell her what the outside world was like, as they were not allowed to leave the house or have friends. They couldn't even play outside with the neighbors. Sometimes we would see them through the window jumping rope or playing. The happiest time I could experience was at school. There was a nun who gave us Religion and Catechism classes. One day, I asked her how I could become a nun, to be in a calm and quiet place. She simply answered: -If you serve as a nun, then I will serve as a Bishop-. Later, in class, the teacher asked who knew the one in this picture, which was an image of the Divine Master.

Quickly, a little girl answered: Me: he was the one who hugged me and hid with me behind the sofa when my parents were fighting. I came to imagine that this little girl was suffering more than us, and God manifested Himself to her to show her that He is everywhere, He is watching and protecting us. That little girl's parents died in that fight and now she lives with foster parents.

Esperanza could not understand why this father, after spending so much time with other women, having children and other homes. I would ask her: why is he coming to this home and why did Alicia let him come to abuse her, use her and get her pregnant again? She said she could not deny him entry because he would destroy the house, break the windows or if she called the police, they would take him to jail and after two months they would release him and he would come to kill her or continue beating her. Anyway, one day when he came home, I don't know what was the reason for the fight, we never knew the causes of the disagreements, I had to witness that while Alicia was pregnant, already 7 or 8 months old, he threw her to the ground and kicked her all over. That day I said to myself: I will not forgive him.

We could watch very little television, and sometimes listen to the radio on certain stations. Rock music was not allowed; Alicia said that this was music for marijuana users and that if she found out that we were listening to this music, she would break our radio. When she went out on an errand, we, among siblings, would designate someone as sentinel in turn to let us know when she was coming back, so we could turn off the radio. We enjoyed listening and dancing to that music.

Every night, I would look at the stars through my window; their bright sparkles seemed to convey to me a message of hope. Despite the adverse circumstances, I dreamed of a different future, far from the gloom that surrounded me. Marriage presented itself as an opportunity to forge my own destiny, to take control of my life and seek the light I longed for.

Then I understood that I could only get out of that 'House' by getting married, I say 'house' because it could not be called a home. But I would not allow myself to be married to the man those dysfunctional parents wanted, as they did with my older sisters.

CHAPTER 2

Marriage as an Opportunity

One July 20, Colombia's Independence Day, we went with Alicia and my younger brother to the parade. We were there trying to see through the people when a very attentive gentleman came over to help me lift my little brother up to a window so he could see better. Alicia thanked him for his kindness and courtesy, and in turn we looked at each other....

He asked Alicia, begging for a ride home in his car, and she agreed. Then, he started asking us out and/or out to eat. His car was a nice long Buick, with soft music playing on his tape deck. Those restaurants were like the mansions Alice had described to me of her ancestors' palaces. Once again I began to dream, to fantasize.... One day she called me in the afternoon and told me: 'When you have a chance, go to the front yard and pick up a package I left'. I went and found some very fine chocolates and a doll; it was a very elegant Barbie with a dress-coat-and-hat outfit. When I called to thank her, she told me that I was prettier than that doll and that she dreamed of being able to give me a dress just like the doll, a blue and white one.

Well, the days went by and Alice was restless because our customs did not include receiving gifts often. However, when he came back to visit, he brought with him another gift, a pearl ring. To this day, I have never seen its beauty and simplicity again.... Alicia took the opportunity to ask him: 'What is the meaning of this gift? Let me explain that our customs differ significantly from those of the people with whom you probably interact on a regular basis.

It is important for you to understand that our way of life is unique and has particular traditions that we have preserved over time. My daughter is not for sale, if that is what you are looking for. Here, our daughters have come to the altar as virgins. It is not customary for a daughter to be visited for years, spending time without commitment. Here, whoever visits a daughter does so with the word of marriage and a definite date. My daughters are not those who have casual friends.

Then she asked him with that ring, is he asking her to marry him? He blanched and said, 'I would love to be able to say yes... but right now, my father recently passed away and I have the whole burden on my shoulders: the business, my mother and my two sisters. I can't get married right now, but maybe in a year's time I can'. Alice immediately replied, 'We must return all the gifts to you and, if when you can and she is available, then it will be different. He begged her to please allow him to enjoy the gifts while he could return, and she agreed.

After that meeting, I never crossed paths with him again. My heart was sinking in sadness, but at the same time, it clung to the hope of seeing him again someday.

One of my brothers, who no longer lived at home and had his own home, would say to me, 'Run away with him.... I'll help you...' But was that appropriate? He was a very proper man and he wasn't suggesting that I get married, was he?

One day when I could not attend school because we had been sent back home for not paying the monthly fee, Alicia got a job for me at a bank to help out financially at home. I liked the idea; it was like an answer to the hope I had placed in God through my prayers.

The bank bus would pick me up at the corner of my house in the morning and drop me off at the same place in the afternoon. The job was simple: I counted old bills to remove them from circulation and then they were burned. Over time, I gained strength and psychological courage and decided to call him. Despite being shy, insecure and immature, hearing his voice paralyzed me. His sweet words echoed in my mind and From that day on, every day at my lunch hour, he would call me at 12:00 p.m. The office phone would ring and for a while we would only talk on the phone. Then he asked how he could see me for even 5 minutes, I replied that he could just meet me at the door of the bank and walk to where the bus was parked to take me home. He nodded and said 'Okay'.

We walked that way together; the building in front of the bank had a passageway that led to another street with stores, so we decided to walk that way. As we walked through, we just looked at each other and smiled.... There were people coming and going when suddenly I saw my father in front of me. Since I hadn't been home in a while, such was my confusion, mixed with fear and hatred, that I didn't know what to do. It all happened so fast that he didn't stop and I continued walking, already frustrated at what was about to happen. When I arrived home, Alicia was ready as always, with her charged angry expression, and without saying a word, she handed me a piece of paper. It was a letter of resignation from the bank, thanking me for the job opportunity. She had me sign it and the job was over. And not content with the signed resignation, she vociferated that my father had told her how much she was selling me for, since she even went out alone with the lover.

Since then, I could only cry... I dreamed while listening to ballads on the radio, while taking care of my younger brother. A year passed, when Alicia's best friend invited the whole family to her only daughter's fifteenth birthday party. It was a very big party, with long dresses for the women and men in black tie. I saw many people there, but only one boy who was always alone caught my attention. I saw him in different rooms at different times and he never came out to dance with anyone. I went up to another lounge on the second floor, where there was a very pretty lady talking and looking out of the window towards the other lounges.

It was around 3 o'clock in the morning when Alicia gathered the family to leave. She told me: 'We are leaving, stay here'. At that moment, the lonely boy who was next to me listening to what she was telling me asked her: 'Ah, are you leaving already?' She answered: 'Yes, why?' He said: 'Can I dance with her for a piece before you leave?' Alicia agreed and allowed him to dance with me. Without crossing words, I danced with him. He was young and handsome, he simply said thank you and that was it.

A year later, Alicia's same friend called again to invite us to her daughter's sixteenth birthday party. This time it was not a big party, the young people were just invited to dance for a while. I didn't want to go; nothing motivated me to go out, I just did the housework and prayed in the hope that God would give me wisdom. Alicia had it on her conscience that I had no interest in anything because of her guilt, and she forced me to attend this meeting. There was the lonely boy again. No one was dancing, everyone was talking and drinking rum and Coke. When the mother of the birthday girl arrived, she started taking the boys by the hand and pairing them with the young women so that they could start dancing and the party would take shape.

When she picked up the lone boy, she brought him to me and we began to dance. He talked about general topics, like movies and soccer, among others.

A friend who was with me at the party mentioned to him that there would be a bazaar in the neighborhood the next day. He was present at the bazaar and met the girls who were at the party. He asked them where I lived and went to my house. He spoke to Alicia and asked her permission to call and visit me. Alicia, seeing him so young, immediately said to him:

Hey boy, here we have very different customs from the rest of the people. They don't come here to visit or to warm up the couch. Nobody comes here as a 'friend'. Here, whoever enters is with the word of marriage only. So, let's not waste time talking nonsense, he said. "Well, all right, "I like those customs.

Give me the phone number and I can start visiting him," he asked. Alicia answered: "Only on Sundays". That's how it was. We talked on the phone a lot, but he never said a compliment or a word of love to me. We were like friends, or rather acquaintances. But not even that, because you can't really get to know a person just by talking. Anyway, after two months we got engaged to get married 4 months later.

Alicia felt guilty that I was going to marry that boy. Shortly before the wedding, she called the man she knew I loved and told him to come, that I was getting married and that he was the only one who could stop the wedding. So he came and talked to me, but the absence of that elapsed time made me feel nothing. I didn't even know what I should or had to feel. He came because he was called, not on his own initiative or because he was already willing to marry. I had no idea what was to become of me. However, with the Light of Hope permanently within me and the certainty that God would guide me by filling me with wisdom, I just needed my ticket to 'freedom'."

CHAPTER 3

Renewing My Understanding

Well, you're a married woman now, I thought. Now that you are, what freedom do you think you're going to have? People who get married are the most tied down. You just changed houses and you'll be in a different bondage. I tried not to think, and if I did, it was about doing the opposite of what I had seen Alicia do. I knew that my name was in the Bible, and that Alicia had called me that because she had hoped that I would bring her comfort and some happiness.

That was how my fantasies were materializing; they were recurring and unexpected events. The first was meeting my mother-in-law, that pretty lady whom I met on the second floor of the big Fifteen Years Birthday party. She told me that she had told her son that day to look at me, that she saw a beautiful woman in me, and he answered her:

Yes, she's beautiful enough to put in a window and stare at all day.' Now I knew that maybe that's why she asked me to dance as we were leaving. If the first unexpected event was meeting my mother-in-law, who is not only pretty, fine, elegant and pleasant, but also professes the Christian faith. She taught me the word of God and led me to transformation through the renewal of my understanding.

As I married to leave home, I believed that this plan was my decision, but as the Light of Hope placed in God illuminated this process of renewal and transformation, I discovered that every moment of our lives is predestined from before the foundation of the world.

What I fantasized about when I read or heard about Jesus' life and all that He had done, was that we could appropriate those promises and live an abundant life, for which He had already paid the price.

My husband is a macho man, very sure of his opinions, I prefer not to use the word stubborn which sounds unpleasant, a career military man, frustrated for having retired from the Naval School due to the death of his father, who was a man of prestige, a doctor, and who brought the first X-ray machines from France to Colombia. He deeply loved his first-born son and spoiled him by giving him everything he could. On some occasions, my mother-in-law told me that her husband overruled her, always giving the reason to his son. I began to analyze the way he had grown up in order to understand his behaviors.

Just as my husband liked the way Alicia had raised me, he wanted to continue taking care of me and jealous of me, watching who I talked to, what I was doing, what I was wearing, etc.

I am grateful to God for giving me the opportunity to know His word, which taught me great and hidden things that I did not know and that, if I have faith, even if it is as small as a mustard seed, it could move mountains.

So I kept practicing every word on Sundays, enjoying the prayer meetings. I felt so different! It was an adventure every day, waiting for the physical manifestations of what I read in the manual of Life, the Bible.

As my wisdom grew and God worked in me, transforming my mind through the renewing of my understanding, I found that as I watched fictional movies, I assimilated the miracles of Jesus in a similar way. If Jesus could accomplish all that seems impossible, magical and supernatural to our minds, I experienced how my faith was strengthened. My thoughts were still filled with wonder, allowing me to keep the fantasy alive. This constant connection between my beliefs, my faith and my hope continued to flourish.

The husband of one of my older sisters remarked to my husband, 'If you want your marriage to last, get away from Alicia's house. She's an absorbing, controlling, hypochondriacal, depressive woman.' He told her yes ... I'd already thought of that, thank you. That advice gave my husband the courage and strength to go now, having our first child, we were going to live in a city on the Atlantic Coast, since I had an uncle and cousins there.

The wife of his uncle was very good to me and gave me an example of strength and positive attitude, she realized that my husband was jealous and did not

Mar del Plata Travel and Tourism Argentina.

Study and Discovery

Author
Samuel Lee

want to share much with the family. He was still the loner I knew.

He would engage in conversations with other people and very quickly come to disagreements. He always wanted to be right and did not want us to attend church. I would contact his mother to prayerfully help me ask God to change, to be a little more flexible so we could attend service on Sundays. The answer came to our hope in God. Then we had our second child; I had wanted a girl, but the mighty and wise God gave me another boy.

All my hope was placed in that supreme being, begging him for wisdom to educate my children. There was a moment when both children were sick, with high fever. The doctor saw them, we gave them medicine and they were still sick. I became desperate and knelt down on my knees, saying, GOD.... If you really listen to me and everything in your word is true, please don't send me any more children'. I didn't want to relive past episodes and I felt helpless not knowing what else to do to get them healed. That was the first covenant I made with my Heavenly Father, or my higher self, as some call it.

Eventually, monotony began to invade my home and a fervent desire to work awakened in me. I longed to experience another miracle in my life, although I knew my husband would not look kindly on me mentioning my thoughts to him. I decided to share my concerns with my mother-in-law and asked her to say a prayer about it. I suggested that, during her conversation with the Divine, perhaps she could weave some hope-filled words to help my desire find its way.

Hallelujah, thank God I didn't have to wait long to get it. Precisely at that time they were looking for personnel for the opening of an important health institution, and they gave me the position of Receptionist. My husband needed to study, and we reached an agreement that he would start studying. Time passed with much sacrifice, and he finally graduated. I was waiting for my chance to do it, I asked him, 'Now it's my turn to study', and he said, 'We'll see when'. I didn't have the opportunity...

While we were working, we agreed to save to buy a car. So we saved, we didn't go out, we didn't eat out, we didn't buy things that weren't basic necessities. After a year, we had the money and he went and bought the car. A few days went by when I asked him, 'When can I get the car? Are we going to take turns for days or weeks?' Then he says, 'What are you saying! Who said a woman can drive?! Now that we have the car and we both saved up to buy it, it turns out that a woman shouldn't drive! Okay!

One fine day I got up early and cautiously, unnoticed, took the car keys and left for the office. It was the first time I had something good to thank my father, who taught me to drive when I was 15 years old. Despite the arguments and the swearing, it didn't matter; he had taught me and at that time it was very important for me to be able to do it.

In my work environment, my coworkers were aware of my husband's sullen attitude. I shared with them that I had taken the car keys without his knowledge and brought it with me. I warned them to be alert, as I expected him to arrive to make a fuss. However, the day passed without incident or confrontation, which left me surprised.

With uncertainty simmering, I returned home wondering what would happen next. But to my astonishment, the result was completely unexpected: God had somehow worked in him. Despite my expectations, when I got home, he didn't utter a word on the subject and, to my surprise, never used the car for himself again. Even on weekends, he took it upon himself to wash and polish it, making sure it was spotless for me to enjoy. At that moment, I remembered with conviction that Christ lives and that God truly cares for me.

CHAPTER 4

In the Shadow of Drug Trafficking

While in the city ranked as the most dangerous in the world, my husband received an appointment as a judge in the Force of Order, an institution where the shadow of the Mafia was deeply infiltrated. Within those corridors, even among the highest ranks, orders were woven in flagrant violation of the law, testing the integrity of all those involved.

They offered him a lot of money to do it, but my husband, although he had a rough character, was a very responsible, honest and loyal man. He used to say: 'If we have to drink only panela water because there is no more, it doesn't matter, we drink it with a clear conscience. That is the important thing.

As he did not allow himself to be bought, one day the highest-ranking person of that institution came to his office to tell him that he was fired from his job. He knew that it was not the function of that person to fire him, since judges are appointed or removed by the President of the Republic himself, but he could not do anything else but leave. A few days later we were in the car, he would take me to my work, when I felt a thunderous sound. It was two men on a motorcycle shooting at my husband and the bullets were passing close to me as well. My wounded husband let go of the wheel. I, from the other seat, as best I could, swerved the car towards a house and my husband managed to brake. When I turned the car around to get him out, I stopped a passing cab. I only took his briefcase because I knew it contained very important documents.

We went to the nearest hospital. There, the emergency doctor took his vital signs, asked him questions and he answered them. At no time did he lose consciousness. I said to the doctor, 'Why don't you take him to surgery or intensive care?' The doctor says, 'Ma'am, he's consistently fine; you're the one who needs medical attention. We can't do anything to your husband here. If you want, I'll lend you an ambulance and take him to another hospital. I said, Yes, thank you.

We went to another hospital. When we arrived, the receptionist said, you have to leave a deposit of $30,000 pesos. My mind told me, that's impossible, we never have that amount in our pocket. However, I reached into her wallet and took out exactly $30,000 pesos. We were experiencing a supernatural episode. Then they say, A scanner. They put him in a machine that looked at his whole body inside. You could see that one bullet entered through his temple and deflected behind his nose without hurting him. The other entered through the left side and exited through the back. My thoughts were: 'What marksmanship those men had, well trained, riding on a moving motorcycle while our car was also moving forward!' My mind kept repeating: 'One bullet entered through the temple, and the other, which was headed for the heart, entered slightly higher and exited through the back without causing any damage?

Now, a disturbing question arises: if law enforcement is meant to safeguard citizens, what happens when those same forces are aligned in the opposite direction? My mind raised deeply disturbing questions about trust and balance in our society.

I felt like I was floating, I wasn't scared or anxious. Like when I was a child, I was just observing what was going on around me. There was something inside me that was in control of everything, life. Jesus said: I am the way, the truth and the life. All human beings have it within us and if we hear his voice, we give him the opportunity to fill us with his love that exceeds all knowledge.

While my husband was being scanned, I waited outside. At that moment, a high-ranking officer approached, his face reflecting concern and compassion. Turning to me, he asked, Are you the wife? I want to congratulate you, your husband was unharmed, I knew everything that was really going on.

After entering the room, I peeked into the hallway and discovered a man sitting like a guard by the door. The situation became tense: how could we escape now that they had us in their sights? It was obvious that they had already found out that he did not die in this attack. I stood silently inside the room, feeling the uncertainty envelop me. At that moment, a gentleman enters with confident steps and his gentle gaze reassures me. His words echo in the air: 'Don't worry, trust me,' he assured me serenely.

Picking up the phone, he dialed a number and struck up a conversation with my sister-in-law's husband. I recognized his voice instantly; it was the same family member who held the position of vice president in a very large company. I discovered to my astonishment that this gentleman who was with us was the head of security for that company and that is why he sent him to help us get out of there.

I can't find words big and deep enough to express my gratitude to God. That morning, before leaving home, my oldest son uttered some momentous words: 'I'm going to accompany you because I have a guitar lesson'. I replied that it was too early and it would be better if it was later. The light of hope in God continued to illuminate my path, my home and embrace my children. If it were not for the power and greatness of God, my son would not be with us today, as several bullets were embedded in the back seat that would have taken his life.

CHAPTER 5

Facing the Reality of Drug Trafficking

As we witnessed in the previous chapter, on the morning of that tragic day, we left our home as usual, as my husband was taking me to work, only to find ourselves unable to return. Thanks to the Light of Hope placed in God, once again His power manifested itself through my sister-in-law's husband, who sent us that angel expert in security, and that same night he took us out of the hospital, taking us directly to the airport, we entered an ordinary commercial airplane, occupying the interior with our presence as the only way to get to the airport, When we landed if it was at the airport but I noticed that it was on the dark runway, an ambulance and other cars were waiting for us, maybe private security, they took us directly to the hospital, I realized that they did not talk to anyone like the receptionist or orderlies, everything was secretly ready.

After leaving the hospital, upon arriving at my sister-in-law's house, we were surprised to learn that both my brother-in-law and one of my brothers had embarked on an overland journey to the city where we were staying. Their goal was to rescue our children. The next day, we were finally reunited, our children safe and in the company of family.

In sync with my sister-in-law's husband sending the security man, a truck was on the move with its team of helpers, in charge of moving our belongings. Meanwhile, I remained immersed in a state of awe, simply observing how the majesty of Christ was being revealed all around me, making us feel enveloped in His love, which surpasses knowledge.

My mother-in-law was just moved to a new apartment, not even she knew her new phone number, when she rings and she answers, they tell her: We already know that your son did not die, but tell her that we have his location and that of her other children as well.

She was the one who taught me the word of God, anguished she tells me: If we have to live more episodes like this or perish, may his will be done, he makes everything perfect.

Days, weeks and years went by without any news of those murderers. However, in the news, a different panorama was revealed: the inhabitants of the city, catalogued as 'the most dangerous in the world', found themselves plunged into despair before the horror that harassed them, being victims of what was supposed to be the force of order, they had probably taken the law of defense in their hands, because the corpses of several young people belonging to that institution were found in different areas of that city.

CHAPTER 6

All that Happens is for the Best

Now that we have lived so many strong experiences, but with Him, in Him, and for Him, I studied to obtain the "Personal Life Coach" Certificate so I can help others to live to the fullest, so they can see the Light of hope in God and be born again, in the Spirit.

Since then, I have nurtured the aspirations of women, men and children alike, strengthening their confidence so they can realize and pursue their hopes and dreams. I have encouraged them to put their talents and skills into action, empowering them to fulfill their goals and objectives in a meaningful way.

Listening to the situations that these people live, I told them that problems do not exist, that the problem is what you think of it, they are situations or personal experiences that we must look at from different angles, to be able to fix them with wisdom and love, to improve our daily life, as long as we are aware of formatting the cassette, "our mind and heart", this means that we get rid of our past, of all the bad treatments, frustrations and attachments.

Putting into action the Faith and Hope placed in God, being born again (John 3:3).

That Light of Hope kept illuminating my soul and the situations that my clients were experiencing, were so strong and painful, that I could see that what I had lived in my childhood was good and easy to bear if we compare. Seeing cases of drug addicted sons, other rebels disrespecting their parents, daughters raped by their own parents, others prostituting themselves, others selling marijuana, young couples having children, all these situations are the result of the lack of courage of the parents to educate them with love and respect, protect them and discipline them.

I began to give infinite thanks to God for Alicia, my mother, who protected all her children, disciplined them, took care of them from bad company, taught them to respect every person, to clean the house, to be responsible for their duties, that if we started something we should finish it, that if we commit ourselves to a task or a job, we should do it conscientiously because the greatest satisfaction is that of fulfilled duty.

Grateful to the Light of Hope in God, who put in my path Francisco Navarro Lara who made possible the publication of this book and that when reading his book Master Mind, I found this paragraph:

"The good news is that there is nothing to forgive, the decisions we make in life are the ones that have to be; we have to be here and now without feelings of guilt and not let them make us feel guilty."

I also learned that what I judged as bad, strong or terrible was the gymnasium of life, God put those people to be our teachers, to form our character and grow to the measure of the perfect man. And to become pure love in action, to be his temple, his vehicle in which he moves to reach his elect, because many are called and few are chosen.

Remembering what Wayne Dyer taught us about: if you squeeze an orange juice comes out, what comes out is what is inside. You can apply the same logic with you when someone squeezes you, pressures you, or tells you something unpleasant or criticizes you and you get angry, hate, bitterness, tension, depression or anxiety that is what is inside, if what you want is to give and receive love and happiness, change what you have inside and change your life.

If we seek that change, we must make it a habit in our daily life, every positive phrase that we find, of everything guarded, guard your heart because from it life flows.

Yes, dear readers, we have to listen and believe our Heart... This is exactly what we must do, take care of how we are thinking and feeling, it is something like loving ourselves, valuing ourselves, educating ourselves, knowing and letting out all the wonderful gifts and talents with which God sent us to this world; not for us to walk in and with the world, only so that He through us can finish His work, to achieve BEING, which is much better than HAVING.

CHAPTER 7

Discovering True Freedom

And you shall know the truth and the truth shall set you free.

To the extent that we are aware that Jesus Christ is risen and His Holy Spirit is within us and we are born again, we are permanently connected to Him, nothing can separate us. For every morning we are new creatures, filled with His love and wisdom, which makes it evident that we are no longer victims of our own opinion, nor do we allow ourselves to be driven by our emotions, nor do we allow the actions of others to interrupt our inner peace. People do things and it is up to us to decide whether they affect us or not.

We already know that by grace we are saved, Jesus preached to us the gospel of the kingdom of God, and that is the paradise in which he wants us to live, it is living the here and now, valuing and enjoying every moment, being grateful for the permanent miracle of being alive, the fact of dawning in perfect balance and understanding, we can see, hear, think, walk. Our organs acting in harmony with each other without stopping!

Yes, we must live each day as if it were the last, because we do not know if the next day we will be or not. Looking and detailing that what we qualify as insignificant things are those little things that lead us to the knowledge of the great the true and that is what makes us live rejoicing, which means to be fully happy.

Hope means: 1. confidence that what is desired will occur or be achieved. 2. object or person in which one trusts to obtain what is desired.

I analyzed that Hope is similar or the same as Faith, the certainty of what is hoped for the conviction of what is not seen. Therefore, Hope is Faith in action.

So "Hope or Faith ends where worry begins and worry ends where Hope or Faith begins". (Author's phrase unknown)

I would tell my friends... someday I will live in the United States, I will learn to speak English, I will be near the sea and I will marry a Gringo with blue eyes, who will pamper me, who will say romantic words to me, who will cook for me, who will help me with the chores, they would laugh, make fun and tell me, Esperanza, you are still a child, a dreamer, you never mature, that does not exist! I told them: if God has done such great miracles in my life, why He is not going to do an easier one for me, how to help me fulfill that dream.

Remember the true freedom is in the mind, you can be locked in a cell, but feeling free, it is the body, the flesh, the physical, the temporal, the temporary, the limited, but the eternal, the true and limitless is in the Spirit.

In my next book I will tell you my dreams come true....

Here is my favorite verse "Delight yourself in the Lord and he will give you the desires of your heart" (Psalm 37:4).

See you next time!

Biography of

Esperanza Gutiérrez Piñeros

I am not a "manager", but a **COACH**... a **MENTOR**.

Born in Colombia, South America, Esperanza Gutiérrez Piñeros is a descendant of Spanish aristocracy. She has followed her dreams and aspirations to help others. She studied Human Resource Management and obtained her Bachelor's Degree in Human Talent Development. She is a Troop Leader for the Girl Scouts of the United States. She received a certification as a Personal Life Coach from the International Coaching Research Group.

She raised three ambitious and successful children (two boys and a girl). Thanks to the love and respect she received from her children as a result of her role as a MOTHER, but more importantly, as a FRIEND and CONFIDENT, they unconsciously became her coaches, motivating her to achieve her own goals.

Esperanza has consistently nurtured the aspirations of women, men and children alike, increasing their confidence to fulfill their hopes and dreams by putting their talents and abilities to work.

Her hobbies include reading, traveling, working, building friendships and altruism, all done with love and commitment. He also enjoys reading the Bible, as well as books by Wayne Dyer, Anita Moorjani, Louise Hay, Joe Vitale, Don Miguel Ruiz and Deepak Chopra. Through these authors, she discovered that what she was doing on a recurring basis already had the foundation of a 'Professional Life Coach'. For this reason, she decided to increase her knowledge and study hard for the time necessary to obtain the above-mentioned certification. She has guided many people, individually and in groups, including housewives, children, adolescents, couples and families, through various situations such as behavioral problems, depression, self-esteem.

Contact: esperanzagupi@gmail.com

Facebook Esperanza Gutierrez Piñeros

Made in the USA
Columbia, SC
31 October 2023

24800462R00028